Nature's Nightmares

Haydn Middleton

Ginn

Living Nightmares

For centuries, they've been spreading terror, panic, death and destruction across the face of the earth. They come with no warning and in a matter of moments they'll turn your whole world upside down. What are they? Monsters? Aliens? No, they are killer winds, horrific hailstorms, erupting volcanoes, lightning bolts, frightening floods and murderous earthquakes – all freak attacks from Mother Nature!

As you quiver under your quilt reading about these nightmares of nature, write down and keep your answers to each **QUIZ** question. (Remember, the answers are in the book!) Are you ready to be blown, blasted and shaken?

Take Cover!

Sky Bullets

The horrors of hailstorms!

Great Shakes

Hold on tight as the earth moves under your feet!

Something in the Air

yuk!

cough!

cough!

Hold your breath as a choking cloud descends!

Sky Bullets

You'd be stunned by some of the things that rain down from above. On a hot summer's day in 1984, the people of Munich, Germany were literally stunned by the downpour! With no warning, a bombardment of icy bullets rained down on the city. The 'bullets' were hailstones, but not normal pea-sized hailstones. These monsters were almost ten centimetres and hurtled to earth at nearly 100 miles per hour!

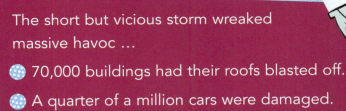

The short but vicious storm wreaked massive havoc …

- 70,000 buildings had their roofs blasted off.
- A quarter of a million cars were damaged.
- A Boeing 757 aircraft had holes bored in it (luckily it was not flying at the time!).
- Crops in fields outside the city were smashed flat.

What a NIGHTMARE!

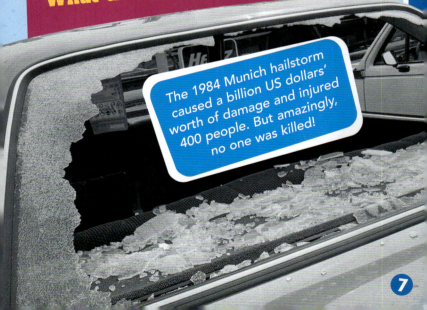

The 1984 Munich hailstorm caused a billion US dollars' worth of damage and injured 400 people. But amazingly, no one was killed!

MOTHER NATURE'S
Record Breakers

The world's largest recorded hailstone fell in Bangladesh in 1986. It weighed a whole kilogram – that's as heavy as a bag of potatoes! The thought of this falling on your head is enough to keep anyone awake at night!

FiRiNG BaCK FaCT

About a century ago, British farmers fired shots from special anti-hailstone guns into nasty-looking storm clouds. They hoped to stop nightmare hailstones from forming, then raining down on their crops. It never worked – and when the shots dropped back down they often wounded onlookers!

A hailstone grows as it gathers ✲✲✲✲✲ of ice

So how do these monstrous hailstones get to be so big?

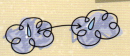

1 If a frozen raindrop finds itself in a certain type of storm cloud, it is tossed up and down at high speeds.

2 As the raindrop pings back and forth, more and more coats of ice gather on it – like the layers on an onion!

3 Eventually it gets too heavy to stay in the air, so it plummets to the ground – and on to you!

Great Shakes

You expect to be shaken about on a rollercoaster, but not when you are at home having your lunch! Just before noon, on an otherwise ordinary day in 1923, the city of Tokyo in Japan was shaking where it stood! In streets and houses across the city, over two million people felt the earth trembling beneath them. The earthquake lasted just ten minutes, but then the real nightmare started … Buildings started falling down!

Many homes caught fire and these fires could not be put out because the earthquake tremors had wrecked the city's water pipes. Half the city burned down and more than 140,000 people were killed.

MOTHER NATURE'S
Record Breakers

Japan is an unlucky record breaker – it has had more major earthquakes than anywhere else in the world! In 1995, a massive shake, which lasted only 20 seconds, killed over 5,000 people in the Japanese city of Kobe and left more than 300,000 people homeless.

FReaKY FaCT

The day before the earthquake in Kobe, many people saw spooky blue lights in the sky. Scientists think that energy under fault-lines creates a strong electric charge above ground – and this electricity produces these 'warning' lights!

QUIZ When plates in the earth's crust grind togethe

So what makes the earth shiver and shake?

1 The earth's crust is made up of huge 'plates'.

2 These plates are always moving – very slightly, and very slowly.

3 When these plates grind together, they set off shock waves.

4 We feel these shock waves as violent tremors on the earth's surface.

Earthquake!

Something in the Air

1 In 1952, most people living in London had smoky coal fires. Coal-burning power stations made the air even smokier. One foggy, windless day, this smoke started to build up and up inside cold, damp air …

2 All this smoke mixed in with the fog to become 'smog': a thick greenish-yellow murk, flecked with sooty black particles.

3 For five days, the filthy smog hung over the city, making it hard to see more than a metre ahead. For people with heart or lung problems, breathing it in proved fatal … Hundreds died, then thousands – and London's undertakers ran out of coffins!

4 At last a wind arrived and shifted the smog. London could be seen again! To stop any more smog nightmares gripping the city, members of Parliament voted to make London a smoke-free zone.

Water Slaughter

If it rained on your birthday party, you'd be very annoyed. Well, the people of Big Thompson Canyon were more than just annoyed when the rain started to pour on their party in the summer of 1976 – they were petrified! That year, the American state of Colorado was 100 years old and so 3,000 partygoers were in Big Thompson Canyon, celebrating in style. But at 6p.m., a thunderstorm struck and the skies opened up. Nearly a year's worth of rain cascaded down in just one evening!

Because it all happened so fast, it was called a 'flash' flood. Fifty million tons of water roared down the canyon, bulldozing mud and rocks into a great surging wall!

This awesome wall of mud and rocks was six metres tall, and destroyed everything in its path, including over 400 homes.

MOTHER NATURE'S
Record Breakers

Why is China a world record breaker? Well, history's worst floods have all struck China! In 1332, massive rainfall burst the banks of the Yellow River, flooding such a vast area that about seven million people were drowned.

FuTuRe FaCT

Our world keeps getting warmer – and as water heats up, it expands. If sea levels continue to rise, coastal cities all over the world will be in danger of flooding. If the polar ice caps melt too, we're in serious trouble!

So how do flash floods start?

1 Thunderstorms often bring heavy rain, but winds usually blow it over a wide area.

2 If it's a very still day, however (like on a warm summer's day!) the storm will stay in the same place.

3 All the rain will keep pounding down on the same spot … **flash flood!**

Hit and Twist

Imagine a gigantic pair of hands reaching down to your house from the sky. The right hand savagely wrenches the building in one direction while the left hand just as savagely wrenches it the opposite way. Your house is torn apart! That's what it's like to be caught in the grip of the world's most **ferocious whirling wind**: a tornado!

Some tornadoes – or twisters – are up to 100 metres wide – so it's hard to escape the nightmare of a tornado if you live in its path!

In March 1925, a nightmare tornado raced for 220 miles across the middle of the USA. A great roaring funnel of cloud smashed through whole towns at a speed of 60 miles per hour – killing 689 people and hurling bodies more than a mile away into the nearby countryside! In under four hours, the tornado left 11,000 people without homes.

MOTHER NATURE'S
Record Breakers

In 1881, during a violent storm, a mass of sea crabs fell from the sky on the streets of Worcester – more than 25 miles away from any coast! How did this happen? Well, tornadoes which travel over the sea can turn into amazingly powerful 'waterspouts'. As well as water, they can suck up sea creatures and even small boats, carry them off, and later drop them to the ground!

FaLSe MoNSTeR FaCT

From a distance, some waterspouts look like beasts with large heads and snake-like necks rising up from the deep. Have you ever heard of the Loch Ness Monster? Maybe this monster is, in fact, just a waterspout seen moving back and forth across the Scottish loch's surface!

Fish & Chips

I wanted Fish & Chips, **NOT** Fish & Ships!

So what causes these terrifying twisters?

1 Inside thunder clouds, warm wet air can be sucked up to meet cold dry air.

2 The two types of air rub together in a corkscrew motion.

3 This creates a violent wind that spins so fast and furiously, it sucks up whatever it whirls across!

Blow Outs

If the ground beneath your feet had been shaking for months, you'd be having sleepless nights, wouldn't you? Well, this is what happened to thousands of people living under Mount Pinatubo in the Philippines – and they were getting twitchy! Then the mountain started to bulge, with streams of gas fizzing out. Mount Pinatubo had been a volcano once, but locals were sure it was extinct. But this big, bad volcano wasn't extinct – it was just sleeping …

Nothing to worry about here!...

On the afternoon of 15 June 1991, Mount
Pinatubo erupted. For nine devastating hours, it
vomited vast cauliflower-shaped columns of ash,
gas and steam 34 kilometres up into the air.
Great avalanches of lava flowed down its slopes.
Nearly a thousand people were killed, 8,000
homes were destroyed and 75,000 more were
damaged. Nightmares don't come much nastier.

MOTHER NATURE'S
Record Breakers

In 1815, Mount Tambora in Indonesia blew its top and gave the whole world a record breaking nightmare! The volcano shot so much gunk up into the air that it reduced its own height by 1,400 metres! But more seriously – a filthy veil of ash spread around the world, reducing sunlight and cooling the temperature. It was still playing havoc with the climate the next year when snow fell in the eastern USA in *June!*

FReaKY FieLD FaCT

In Mexico in 1943, a crack suddenly appeared in a field of corn. Smoke gushed up, then ash and rocks spurted out – followed by piles of red hot lava. One week later, a brand new 150 metre volcano was standing where crops had once grown!

So what makes a volcano blow its top?

1 Many volcanoes are cone-shaped hills or mountains with a hollow passage running through their middle.

2 These passages reach right down beneath the earth's crust.

3 If hot bubbling rock and gases under the earth's crust break through, they can rush up one of these passages – and **explode** out of the volcano's summit.

Lightning
Fact and Fiction

 TRUE or FALSE? Lightning never strikes the same place twice. **False**

The Eiffel Tower in Paris, for example, is struck 20–30 times a year! Lightning usually seeks out the highest object around – so it's risky to shelter under tall trees during storms!

TRUE or FALSE? Lightning can blast the nose-cone off an aeroplane in mid-flight. **True**

It happened in 1979, on a flight between St Louis and Indianapolis in the USA. Incredibly, the aeroplane made a safe emergency landing, with no harm to the 74 people on board.

Lightning can turn a desert cactus into a bomb. True

A cactus is full of water and this turns to steam when struck by lightning. It then explodes, showering sharp spines everywhere!

Lightning set one of the world's greatest cities on fire in 1997. True

The city that went up in smoke was Sydney in Australia. A bolt of lightning set fire to the very dry bushland around Sydney's suburbs, and then high winds blew the flames into the streets!

MOTHER NATURE'S
Record Breakers

In the USA, about 150 people are killed by lightning strikes every year. But between 1969 and 1977, Roy Sullivan, a National Park Ranger in Virginia, USA, was hit by lightning an astonishing *seven* times. His eyebrows were burnt once, and his hair caught fire twice – but he suffered no major injuries!

FLaMiNG FaCT

Lightning heats the air as it makes its leap from cloud to cloud, or to the ground. It can heat the air up to 30,000°C! That's so hot that when lightning strikes sandy soil, it melts it at once!

Not again!

So what exactly is lightning?

1 Lightning is a build-up of electricity inside a cloud.

2 The electricity then leaps in a powerful flash to another cloud, or from the cloud to the ground.

3 At the same time as the natural electricity makes its leap, a flash of light is given off.

Well it's safe to go to sleep now: Nature's Nightmares have gone away – for the time being! Did you get all these answers to the quiz questions? Now, juggle with the first letters of all six answers to make a word for something we'd all do during one of Nature's Nightmares.

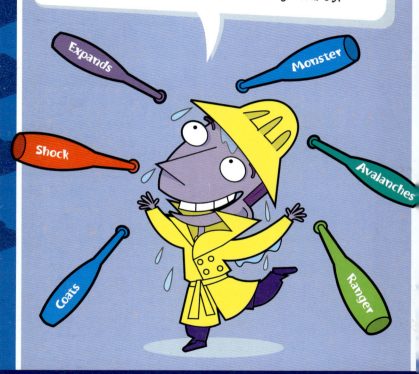

Expands

Monster

Shock

Avalanches

Coats

Ranger

The first letters CSEMAR make SCREAM!
Watch out for Nature's Nightmares!